A GUIDEBOOK TO PERFECT HEALTH

THE NEW ME

GAGAN DHAWAN

BOLD

An imprint of
Srishti Publishers & Distributors

Srishti Publishers & Distributors
A unit of AJR Publishing LLP
212A, Peacock Lane
Shahpur Jat, New Delhi – 110 049

editorial@srishtipublishers.com

First published in India by Bold,
an imprint of Srishti Publishers & Distributors in 2024

10 9 8 7 6 5 4 3 2 1

This is a work of non-fiction, based on the authors' experiences and life-learnings. It provides practical solutions to everyday problems, but the recommendations given herein are in no way intended to be a substitute for professional advice and help.

Disclaimer: While the author and publisher have utilized their earnest attempts in setting up this book, they make no portrayals or guarantees regarding the exactness or fulfilment of the substance of this book. The guidance and procedures contained in this may not be reasonable for your circumstances. Expert guidance and discretion is advised. The recommendations given herein are in no way intended to be a substitute for professional advice and help.

Printed and bound in India

CONTENTS

ACKNOWLEDGEMENTS

I am grateful to the Almighty for His blessings and invaluable support. I owe thanks to many professionals and associates without whom this book would not have been possible. I thank my medical advisers, Dr Nandita Shah, Founder, Sharan (Sharan-India.org) and a recipient of the Prestigious Nari Shakti Award 2016; and Dr Swati Kedia Gupta, a clinical psychologist and the author of the *Quit Tobacco* book from The New Me series.

My gratitude will always be towards Aditya Arora for his valuable inputs on physical training. He's a PTA Global Certified Personal Trainer and holds many other international fitness training certificates, including a Les Mills Instructor Rehab Essentials certification.

I am grateful for the time and advice of Sheetal Sawhney, the author of the *Yoga* book (also part of The New Me series) and a certified Yoga trainer from the Ministry of AYUSH and Sri Sri School of Yoga; and Radhika Sharma, the co-author of this book as well as a social worker and an educator. This book also benefitted from the advice of Nupur Gupta, a nutrition and fitness consultant.

Senior legal advisor Hemant Shah and lawyer Namrita Pahwa were generous with their support. I would like to mention Tarunima Bajpai (founder of EcoSwop Solutions and a lawyer, animal rights activist, and environmentalist) for leading this project with her passion and hard work.

Last but not the least, my comrade-in-arms, Ravi Dutta, thank you for always being there for me.

**Take care of your body.
It's the only place
you have to live in.**

Jim Rohn

Gagan Dhawan

A NOTE FROM THE AUTHOR

A few years back, my health had hit an all-time low. I was not just in poor shape, but also quite unhealthy. There comes a time when you realize discipline has to be given utmost importance. For me, this was it! When I was advised to start taking heavy doses of medicines for cholesterol and blood pressure to avoid dire consequences, I knew I couldn't waste any more time. This round of medical tests was an eye-opener for me. The helplessness of not being in control directed me towards research. With days of tedious research and consultancy with many experts, both in India and abroad, I learnt that there was no going back once you started taking medicines for cholesterol or blood pressure.

I decided to get my act together. I asked myself, "If not you, then who would put in efforts for your health?" I went on a 90-day routine for health and wellness change. I shifted to a plant-based diet and began to make small but significant changes in my lifestyle- such as getting into an exercise routine, sleeping/ waking up on time, and consuming a lot of fluids. After 3 months of following this new pattern religiously, I redid my tests. Lo and behold! I was declared absolutely fit. I no longer needed any medication. Today, I have found that I am addicted to my new and healthier self. And, that is what I want other people to experience.

It might look like just another story to you, but our body can fix itself with a few days of care. Along with hearing what your body needs now, I want people to feel as driven, fit, and full of vitality as I do. This is how the concept of *The New Me* came to life. Ours is a company dedicated towards bringing better health to people. We are driven and motivated by a mission to forge a change in people's lives, by introducing them to wholesome, plant-based food habits and encouraging them to include simple and practical changes in their lives along with some form of daily exercise.

We have begun our mission to make sure we benefit as many people as we can in turning their lives around with this book. It takes a multi-pronged approach to include nutrition and practical workout regimen in your everyday lives. Once you follow the book religiously, you will be able to motivate yourself for sustaining it too.

Compiled under the guidance of the best of consultants and experts, The New Me box of goodness is guaranteed to empower YOU and to change your life for the better. You will see the difference on your face, hair, skin, sexual health, and your energy levels. It goes without saying, the books will also help you to achieve inner peace.

The book propagates fitness tips through suggesting the right fitness tools, workout programmes, diet plans, and various other features. If you are willing to revamp your life and take it to a whole new level, then you are in the right place.

So instead of spending endless hours at the gym or spending money on the latest diet trends, you simply have to follow instructions in this book and transform your body and mind.

So, let's start with the 3-month challenge and commit ourselves to giving it our 100 per cent. The unachievable goals can be your achievements when you invest in your mind and body. Set your eyes on your goal and there will be no looking back.

Be active. Be healthy. Be happy.

Gagan Dhawan

INTRODUCTION

What is *The New Me*?

The New Me is your first step towards a healthy, new life. This book is your very own health kit – it offers a 90-day programme that aims at transforming your mind, body and soul. With the help of our guide books, you will be able to record your journey and jot down daily reviews of your workouts and healthy meal plans.

What Does it Do?

This book is designed to help you develop a balanced lifestyle and attain a healthy weight. You will also be able to tone your body, detoxify, increase bone density, reduce stress, quit smoking, and lead a more mindful existence with clarity of thought and emotion.

When you live a more balanced lifestyle, you make better decisions, personally and professionally. Whether your goal is to lose weight, tone muscles, reduce chronic pain, re-energize, build up your immunity, or just sleep better, you will start feeling and looking your best! This is the idea behind *The New Me.*

Why Do I Need This Book?

Look around a bit. The environment you live is so polluted, not just with pollutants, but also with different toxic energy. This puts a responsibility to make yourself aware and do the most to keep you healthy physically, mentally and emotionally. But before moving onto the 90-day blueprint, let us understand why we emphasize the importance of a healthy mind, body, and soul.

A comfortable and a healthy body enables you to function at a higher order, and be more ambitious. It paves the way for creating a change in a society, whereas a weak body limits your potential and possibility.

We are so caught up with delivering services and meeting deadlines that we forget what we really need. Let us not forget that it is extremely important to take care of our body and mind in order to better care for others.

This book will not only help you to look good and feel good, but will also make you happy and successful. It will help you to master yourself to recreate the hero inside you and become 'the New You'.

Our brain has a gatekeeper which allows only certain thoughts to enter, known as the reticular activating system. So let only positive thoughts enter your mind and put all the negative comments and demotivating thoughts away. You will find yourself in a different space once you are done with the whole workbook. Wondering how? You will have new energy levels, a better outlook, a mind and body makeover – all of which will make you more confident. Your energy levels will be boosted, releasing stress, anxiety, and increasing your focus and attention.

All of us are fortunate in different ways. We take our life for granted. Our able body is an asset and it deserves to be taken care of. Everything we are looking for resides within us. It is time to give your mind-body-soul the highest priority. All you need to do is commit, and adhere to the DIY routine.

I assure you, you'll be thanking yourself that you were committed all this while.

Sleep is the golden chain
that binds health
and our bodies together.

THOMAS DEKKER

01

EARLY TO BED AND EARLY TO RISE

You might have experienced how your body behaves if it's not getting enough sleep. That speaks a lot about the importance of sleep. But why is it so important to have a proper sleep routine? Is it really effective? Or it's just beating around the bush? Is there really any truth to the age-old adage 'Early to bed and early to rise makes one healthy, wealthy and wise'? Let's find the answers.

When someone comes to me for any kind of assistance, I always tell them to 'sleep'. No matter what the problem, sleep is my solution. 'Hey, I need your help. I am not able to prepare for the exam.' 'I am so broke' or 'I am so depressed. My partner broke up with me.' My only advice to all this is, 'Make sure you get enough sleep.' Strange, isn't it?

You may think sleep is not connected to how we deal with our personal or professional problems. However, science has shown us that a good night's sleep (of approximately 8 hours) is the foundation for good health. When we wake up feeling light, fresh and alert, our mind is able to think rationally and take sound decisions. This is but one benefit an individual can experience from regular sleep. Apart from this, there are many involuntary benefits for our mind and body when we improve our sleep cycle, including positive impacts on learning, memory and processing information.[1] That is why the Dalai Lama says, 'Sleep is the best meditation'—it regenerates our brain and physical bodies.

Studies show that a major factor contributing to the success of the rich and powerful is waking up early. It gives them an edge over others. They get to start their day early, organize themselves better and hone their skills, while the majority of the population is still in their beds, dreaming. It is no wonder that only 1 per cent of the population gets to have all the wealth and power.

Waking up early gets you an early advantage over others, where you can utilize the golden hours, working on and planning for yourself and creating a better you. You also become more organized, optimistic, and energetic, which, in turn, can help you reduce your stress levels.

For those of us used to late nights and late mornings, changing our sleep cycle can seem like a difficult task. You might be asking yourself, 'How will a person like me wake up early?' However, as explained by Dr Stuart Pierson,[2] when you wake up early regularly, your body's internal clock, i.e., circadian clock, adjusts automatically and adapts to the new pattern. So much so, that eventually, you won't even require any alarm clock.

Here are a few tips that can help in training yourself to wake up early. As long as there are no underlying sleep disorders such as sleep apnea or parasomnia, these tips have been proven to work.

1. **Get on a sleep schedule.** Go to bed to sleep at the same time every day. Keep an alarm for the same time for the next morning. Stick to this schedule.
2. **Improve your bedtime routine.** A lack of routine is the biggest reason why people find it hard to wake up early. Avoid screen time before you go to sleep as it interferes with sleep. Tempting as it may be to be on your phone or tablet at night, try to switch to reading physical books instead of using a laptop, mobile or tablet.
3. **Avoid napping during the day.** This will allow your

body to slip into sleep in no time at night.

4. **Don't drink caffeine around bed time.**
5. **Keep your alarm clock out of reach** so that you avoid hitting the snooze button.
6. **Eat better during the day.** When your stomach is full and mind is at rest, sleep is peaceful.
7. **Stick to the same schedule on weekends.**

The above steps will make you much more productive. You will have more hours to organize your work, finish your tasks efficiently, and decision-making will be a lot easier.

Early-to-bed-and-early-to-rise takes first place in our manual because of the importance that it holds. It's evident that a mind at peace is much better to call the shots and make important decisions than a tired, over-worked mind.

There is one more aspect related to sleep that is helpful in regulating our schedule. Make sure that you make your bed as soon as you wake up, because that is the first task that you get to do, and once you complete that, it will empower you to finish the rest of your day's tasks. And, no matter how your day goes, everyone loves to come home to a clean and readymade bed.

Z Z Z Z

SUCCESS STORY

JEFF BEZOS

CEO of Amazon;
founder and owner of Blue Origin and Washington Post
(with a net worth of $19,090 crore as of 2021).

Unlike other successful individuals, he mentions that his days aren't rushed and he takes enough time to rest.

"I go to bed early, I get up early," said Bezos. He has been known to prepare and eat a mighty breakfast. He sets most important meetings at the beginning of the day to tackle the biggest problems with a fresh mind. In order to be effective in making decisions, he prioritises his sleep. "Think about it, as a senior executive, what do you really get paid to do?" says Bezos. "As a senior executive, you get paid to make a small number of high-quality decisions. Your job is not to make thousands of decisions every day." [3]

2A

WATER

One of the major sources of life is water, and it impacts our health to a great extent. But how much water should you drink in a day? This seemingly simple question has no simple answer. A common statement we hear is that one needs to drink 7-8 glasses of water every day. But our body is a complex system that changes with time. Thus, the need of water in your body is subjective and individual specific. Factors such as age, gender, and climate you live in, how active you are, pregnancy or breastfeeding influence the need of water in your body. You might not know, but older people, in particular, have been found to not drink enough water as they don't sense thirst as much as the younger ones do.

The human body consistently loses between 2 to 3 litres of water every day through urination, sweating, exhaling water vapours and bowel movement. Those of us who exercise more or live in hotter areas will lose more water from sweating. So we need to replenish the roughly 2 to 3 litres of water that we lose from sweating, breathing and urinating by consuming water, beverages and foods that contain water.[4]

Meeting the daily water requirement

What we need to know is that we get a big chunk of our daily water need from our food and beverages, such as tea and coffee. A good rule of thumb is to listen to your body and drink water when thirsty. As long as you're eating regular meals and fresh fruits, you will meet a significant portion of your daily requirement. Fresh juicy fruits, such as watermelon, and greens such as spinach, cucumber, celery, radish and cauliflower contain a lot of water, so include them in your daily meals.

Benefits of drinking water

Up to 70 per cent of our body is made up of water. Every cell in the human body needs water to work properly.

- Water acts as carrier for nutrients and oxygen to our cells.
- Proper digestion and elimination of wastes through urination, perspiration and bowel movements cannot take place without water.
- It aids normalising blood pressure, regulating body temperatures and stabilizing the heartbeat.
- Water also lubricates and cushions our joints, making our movements easy and smooth.
- It also acts as a protector of our spine and other tissues.

How does insufficient intake of water affect us?

Drinking too little water can affect the smooth functioning of our body. Dehydration happens if we lose more water than what the body takes in. When we're dehydrated, we feel extremely thirsty and fatigued. It can lead to an imbalance in the body's electrolytes such as potassium, phosphate, and sodium. Insufficient intake of water can also cause kidney stones and urinary tract infections. Drinking sufficient water is a simple way to reduce the risk of developing a UTI and to help treat an existing UTI.

So start your day with a glass of lukewarm water. It helps expel wastes from the body and aids digestion. Remember, drink a glass of water whenever you feel thirsty, between meals and before, during and after exercise. Eat fruits that have higher water content to make water consumption tasty and interesting. Watermelon juice, cucumber, lemonade and many other fruit derivatives are great for hydrating the body.

Our food should be our medicine and our medicine should be our food.

2B

HEALTHY EATING HABITS

Our next focus is on a balanced and a healthy diet. The definition of a healthy diet changes as you grow. At times, your diet can also be gender or situation specific. A pregnant woman, for example, requires more folic acid and iron. And the elderly, according to Dr Ami Hall,[5] are advised to consume fewer calories when compared to younger individuals.

One thing is clear: everyone should strive to have a healthy diet, the young or the elderly. It is a must for all individuals who want to lead a healthy and happy life.

When you are happy, your body releases dopamine, also known as the 'happy hormone'. This can be activated by a number of things – meeting friends and family, visiting places, playing games, etc. There are also certain foods, such as banana, avocado and almond, that are known to enhance your mood by releasing dopamine.

There are many benefits of a healthy diet, as stated by the World Health Organization. [6]A nutritious diet helps one maintain weight, boosts immunity, prevents heart diseases, reduces the risk of cancer and obesity, strengthens bones and teeth, increases energy levels and paves the way for healthy development. Healthy eating has more to it than slimming your waistline; it also helps you age better, be more productive, avoid unnecessary and expensive medical care, and, most importantly, prevent psychological and physical stress.

A healthy diet should include fermented foods and foods rich in roughage, fibre, Omega 3, vitamins K, A, B, C, E, calcium, magnesium and carbohydrates. French author François De La Rochefoucauld rightly said, 'To eat is a necessity, but to eat intelligently is an art'. We have simplified that art of eating intelligently for you in our books.

After a lot of research, we have formulated a plan that is easy to follow and not time-consuming. It is economical, nutritious, and healthy for all. However, let's have a look at the meal times one must follow, and other underrated habits.

Breakfast

The only thing worse than a bad breakfast is having no breakfast. There is a reason breakfast is known as the most important meal of the day. Eating breakfast fuels us with vital nutrients and energy. When we wake up, our blood sugar levels, which should be in the normal range for our brains to work at their best, are low, and our body requires re-fuelling. Having breakfast is, therefore, a stepping stone to a fulfilling day and an essential component for making your day fruitful.

A good, healthy breakfast is vital. Avoiding the morning meal can hamper the functioning of your body. So start your day with a hearty and healthy plant-based, whole food diet. It energizes you, gets your mind to work actively and focus better, and enables your brain and body to function better.

Famed American nutritionist Adelle Davis said, 'Eat breakfast like a king' as it keeps you going throughout the day. No matter how busy your day, it is important to never miss your breakfast. Research shows that having a good breakfast also helps in maintaining the right body weight we require. When we eat at appropriate intervals throughout the day, we tend to eat an adequate amount of food, whereas if we skip breakfast, we become prone to overeating. Eating at the right times helps lower what we call 'bad cholesterol' (LDL), improves memory and boosts metabolism.

A healthy diet is a combination of a lot of food groups. For example, carbs give you instant energy, protein provides energy for later and fibres take care of satiation levels, making you feel full. Some quick foods that you can have as breakfast include porridge, wheat breads, muesli, fresh fruits, plant-based yogurt, milk from almonds, oats and soy, smoothies and whole grain granola.

Snacks

Snacks are important for appetite control as they prevent you from overeating before your scheduled meals. It also makes us feel refreshed in the middle of a dull and monotonous day. Taking a snack break will help you focus on work, preventing your energy levels from dipping.

Thus, it is crucial to fuel the body constantly in order to function to the best of one's capabilities. If your energy levels are low in the middle of the day, you can end up feeling restless and irritable and food is all that will be on your mind. Therefore, snack breaks serve as a quick power meal which rejuvenates the body.

Items that you can eat during snack time include whole nuts and seeds, makhana, cereals, bhakarwadi, sandwiches and salads.

Lunch

Lunch is a crucial meal of the day. It gives you the vitality to carry out tasks during the afternoon. A home-made lunch is a good choice in order to consume the necessary nutrients. If you skip any meal in a day, it can cause an imbalance in the body. The daily intake of nutrients and calories can be divided into meals one consumes.

One way of breaking down the consumption of energy can be as follows: breakfast 40 per cent, snacks 10 per cent, lunch 30 per cent, and dinner 20 per cent.[7] A nutritious lunch helps prevent you from eating unhealthy food. On an average, each person requires 2,200 kcal to function well in their personal and professional lives. You can divide the required energy into your meals and snacks to streamline your food intake.

Operating efficiently without providing adequate amount of fuel to the body is not possible. Skipping meals will not just generate intense hunger, but also use up essential fuels like glucose, and cause you to rely on less efficient substitutes.

In order to avoid such trouble, it is essential to come up with a diet chart, keeping in mind not only the most appropriate calorie and nutrient intake, but also how and when to consume your food. Some food items that should be had at lunch include chapatis, brown rice, dal, cabbage, spinach, jackfruit, ragi porridge, etc.

Try to eat your meal in a calm and comfortable ambience and take a minimum of 30 minutes to finish your food. There is a logic behind why our elders ask us to sit and eat, because when we walk or stand and then eat, all the blood supply which ideally should have been in the gut is transferred to our gross motor muscles such as our arms and legs, making us more prone to bloating and indigestion. It is not just what you eat, but how you eat that makes a difference.

Dinner

Although dinner takes up a very a small space in our meal plan, it is equally important to have dinner to witness numerous health and interpersonal benefits explained below. This is the only viable time for most families where all the members can sit together and eat a healthy meal. Studies have shown that having meals together has proven to enhance not just the relationships, but also the taste of the food.[8]

It is important that you eat a healthy (not large) dinner as you won't be eating for the next eight hours approximately. Remember, it is fundamental to maintain a continuous supply of glucose for the smooth functioning of the body at night. A number of people complain of sleeplessness or insomnia and disturbed sleep patterns. Such conditions arise as a result of low sugar levels in the body. This can be curbed by ensuring you have a regular and proper dinner. A good dinner also ends the day on a good note, helping you enjoy a restful and deep sleep. Food items that one can have during dinner include chapatis, dal, green smoothies, capsicum, peas and potatoes, sambar, soya bean, tofu, cauliflower, etc.

Key points to remember whilst having your meals[9]

- Try to have your dinner at least one hour before going to bed or your food will accumulate as fat, making it difficult to digest.
- Avoid fatty foods at night as they are heavy and difficult to digest.
- Eat slowly, in a restful ambience.
- Chew your food well. It makes digestion easier for the stomach.
- Do not skip meals.
- Focus on, and eat home-cooked meals.
- Don't snack right before a meal.
- Every time you eat or drink, remember you are either feeding diseases or fighting diseases. A bad diet can lower immunity; a good diet can boost it. Make the wise choice.

2C

WHOLE FOOD PLANT-BASED DIET

Did you know heart diseases, cancer and diabetes remain the top causes of death, not just in India, but globally?[10][11] And, did you know, we could significantly reduce and reverse the impact of such acute problems just by eating the right diet?

A plant-based, whole food diet can reduce the number of medicines you take by up to 70 per cent [12]and have been known to reverse problems like heart diseases, diabetes, hypertension and other lifestyle diseases.[13][14] Plant-based, whole food diets can have a positive impact on one's lifestyle. It improves the functioning of your brain, making you feel fresh, focused, energetic and positive.

Plant-based, whole food diet is the most talked-about diet globally. But what does plant-based, whole food diet mean? How is it different from being a vegetarian? Most importantly, how can this change of diet occur?

Here, with *The New Me*, we accept that a huge part of the problem is that people who need to settle on the right dietary decisions for themselves and their families are baffled by the options and lack of proper guidance. We will help you bring about a 360-degree change in your life just by switching your diet.

Haven't we heard ample times, 'we are what we eat'! Now just imagine that when you consume meat, chicken, eggs or dairy products, you are also consuming, hurt, as a byproduct. Its result on your health and mind would be disastrous, whereas switching to a plant-based diet would be the most rewarding decision you would ever make in your life. All phytochemicals, antioxidants, minerals and vitamins that you need are found in a plant-based diet.

A whole food plant-based diet can double your energy levels, make you more resilient, help your blood flow smoothly, thereby making you feel light and rejuvenated, boost your confidence and provide a glow to your skin. It purifies our body and mind. As Brahma Kumaris Centre for Raj Yoga says, "If you eat a healthy and cruelty-free diet, you will be more kind and at peace with your soul."[15]

Eat more whole plant foods and less of everything else.

Let us first understand what whole plant-based is and then break down the myths surrounding it.

Whole plant-based diet is a lifestyle.

A way of thinking and method for living which tries to reject – as conceivably and practically as possible – all types of abuse of, and exploitation to, animals for nourishment, or for any other reasons; and by utilising of animal-free options not just to help them but both people and nature. It signifies the act of forgoing all items partially or entirely from animals.[16]

Difference between Vegetarian and Whole Plant-based Diet

Vegetarians are 'almost there' when it comes to being fully plant-based. A plant-based, whole food diet requires only a little effort and is much more rewarding.

The core difference between vegetarians and those who follow a whole plant-based lifestyle is this: vegetarians don't eat animals, but consume animal products (such as milk, eggs and honey); while people who follow a whole-foods, plant-based diet don't just avoid meat, fish and poultry in their diet, but stay away from anything produced using animals (such as milk, eggs and honey). Whole foods refer to natural foods that are not heavily processed (such as whole or minimally refined ingredients).

Myths Surrounding Whole Plant-based Diets[17]

Despite what you might have heard, a plant-based diet can be very beneficial. American dietician Jack Norris propagates that plant-based diets can lower the risks of colorectal and prostate cancer. American physician Michael Greger (in his book *How Not to Die)* discusses how plant-based diets can not only prevent, but also reverse many acute problems. A clean diet can tremendously reduce the risk of chronic diseases, high-blood pressure, high cholesterol, and heart problems. Below, we bust some myths surrounding plant-based diets.

• Practising whole plant-based diet is expensive

A common misconception about whole-foods, plant-based diet is that practising it will put a strain on your wallet. In fact, unprocessed vegetables and whole grains like whole oats and whole wheat are the cheapest options available in the market. Once the food is processed, it becomes a little more expensive. An individual can learn to prepare whole plant-based meals, which will help them make nutritious meals at a low cost.

• Being on a whole plant-based diet is tough

There can be various reasons why something is considered difficult. However, all that is required is the determination to begin and the will power to sustain the lifestyle. There are easily accessible stores and markets which sell plant-based groceries. Once you make the switch to a plant-based diet and experience the results, you would never want to go back.

- **There are limited options for whole plant-based food**

There are thousands of recipes that can be cooked using only plant-based products.[18] These recipes include many different cuisines and consist of a variety of snacks and dishes (such as grilled carrots, soy pulao, chimichurri cauliflower steaks, cucumber melon soup and many more). Most major food chains and restaurants now cater to the growing plant-based population and have incorporated plant-based dishes in their menus, such as Taco Bell's seven-layer burrito fresco style with cinnamon sticks or Pizza Hut's veggie lovers pizza. You see, one has a huge selection to choose from. You can opt for slight modifications and even enjoy your plant-based meals at restaurants.[19]

- **It is difficult for people on a whole plant-based diet to build muscles**

People who are focused on building muscles are generally recommended a low-carb diet, although this philosophy was proven to not be definitive. An 8-week weight-training test was conducted to check the efficacy of a plant-based diet, and the results are eye-opening. People on a normal-carb diet gained 2.9 pounds of muscle mass, whereas those on a low-carb diet had seen a loss in muscle mass. This is because processed types of carbs such as sugar and bread are associated with weight gain whereas unprocessed carbohydrates (such as bananas, legumes, and sweet potato) are responsible for reducing body fat. Mischa Janiec, a professional bodybuilder, sets the perfect example as a plant-based diet follower for maintaining a great physique.

Whole-foods, plant-based diets can be altered as per your requirements, whether those are building muscles, weight management, weight loss, or disease management. If you'd like to look lean and shredded, we've formulated a plan for a plant-based diet that helps in building muscle. You can find it in our meal planning book.

- **It's difficult for people on a whole plant-based diet to lose weight**

Whole-food, plant-based diets have been tremendously effective in losing excess weight faster than any controlled regular diet due to its high fibre and low cholesterol content. In one test conducted by Harvard University, a plant-based diet helped participants lose 4.2 kilos more than people on a controlled diet, over an 18-week study period.[20]

However, plant-based diets require the right planning in order to get the right results. All the help you need to evaluate the right diet for yourself can be found in our meal planning workbooks, including the right ways to cook plant-based meals and some mouthwatering recipes.

Why Go Whole Plant-based?

- **For your own well-being**

Getting your supplements from plant products means creating space for some great alternatives such as whole grains, nuts, seeds and vegetables, and organic products, which are brimming with helpful fibre, nutrients and minerals. Whole-food, plant-based diets have helped in bringing about a holistic change in people's lives.[21]

Protein is an important nutrient for humans. According to Dr Scott Stoll, while both non-vegetarians and whole plant-based diet eaters get to have protein from their respective sources, what animal protein does to the body would shock you.[22]

The repeated consumption of certain red meats can lead to an excess of heme iron and Neu5Gc (a sugar molecule) in our body, which has been linked to inflammation and increased risk of certain types of cancer ; whereas plant-based proteins brings antioxidants, vitamins and minerals that can enhance your overall functioning. Plant protein is said to have 64% more antioxidants than animal proteins, making plant-based diets a better choice without a doubt.[23]

Embracing a whole-foods, plant-based diet improves one's well-being, boosts immunity and even permits individuals to wean themselves off day-to-day medication.

- ## Protecting Animals

Just as humans deserve to live with dignity, so do animals. Just because animals can't communicate verbally doesn't mean they don't feel pain.

Let's suppose a non-vegetarian consumes meat, poultry or fish once a week for a year. That alone accounts for 52 killings. Now let's suppose they eat like this for the next 40 years. That comes to a total of 2,080 killings. The mere idea of killing another creature in order to feed oneself is unkind.

Let us take the milk industry for example. In order to produce milk, cows and buffalos need to lactate, which happens only when they are pregnant. However, in a dairy farm, they are forcefully impregnated through the process of artificial insemination.

When a cow gives birth, the offspring is not allowed to drink its own mother's milk. A male calf is sent to a slaughterhouse immediately, since he is incapable of providing milk and the female calf is tied down and is deprived of milk that was meant for her because all the milk is then commercialized. The industry is nothing like the advertisements you see. In fact, there is a huge amount of pain, suffering and exploitation involved. Please remember, not a single animal goes to a slaughterhouse by will. Things exist in our society due to the cycle of demand and supply. If all of us come together to make a conscious choice to switch to consuming plant-based diets, it can massively reduce the demand for animal meat and animal products, thereby ending our inhumane treatment of them. Let us stop considering animals as commodities. Let's strive to create a compassionate and better world.

- **For the Environment**

Consuming a whole-food, plant-based diet can be the 'single greatest way' to diminish our footprint on the planet. Analysts at the University of Oxford found that reducing the meat and dairy items in one's diet can lessen a person's carbon footprint by up to 73 per cent.

From reusing our home's trash to cycling to work, we all must try to be mindful of our carbon footprints and live a greener life. One of the best things an individual can do to stop environmental degradation is to avoid animal products and live a cruelty-free life.

If a man aspires towards a righteous life, his first act of abstinence is from injury to animals.

Albert Einstein

03

KARMA

One tree can be made into a million matchsticks.
But only one matchstick can burn a million trees!
Circumstances can change at any time.
Don't devalue or hurt anyone in this life.
You may be powerful today,
but time is more powerful than you!

What is Karma?

According to Hinduism and Buddhism, the sum of a person's actions in this and previous states of existence are viewed as deciding their fate in future existences.

Karma means action, work or deed. Karma refers to the spiritual principle of cause and effect, where everything that affects a person is because of something caused by them. The intent and actions of an individual influence the future course of that individual. Good intent and good deeds contribute to good karma, while bad intent and bad deeds lead to bad karma.

The most amazing thing about karma is that you don't know when it will come into force. It could be immediately after you did a good or bad deed, maybe a few years down the line or it may just pass on to your next state of being.

The symbol or motif of Karma is a design of endless knots, symbolizing the interlinking of cause and effect of our deeds. A karmic cycle continues eternally.

Relationship between Karma and a Plant-based Diet

We all know that animals go through suffering just because humans want to eat meat or consume milk.

Yes, we do not ask dairy owners to ill-treat the cow, to impregnate it forcefully or to inject oxytocin to increase the milk supply. But we do pay for this process and encourage them by our demands. An animal doesn't walk into a slaughterhouse on its own. It is confined in a small space. Breeding lives forcefully only to kill them for personal pleasure, or to take away a mother's milk that is meant only for her child will always bring in bad karma.

Everything is a matter of faith. All faiths talk about one factor above all else- kindness and compassion. Whether one believes in God or not, kindness towards others is a fundamental value.

Once you follow a plant-based diet, you give yourself the gift of simplicity. You find it easier to enjoy the little things in life. You know by not eating animals, you are making an impact – at whatever level, you do make a difference. This is Nature's way of maintaining the balance.

It is important for us to believe and act in accordance with the law of karma. Not only will it make the world a better place to live in, but it will also enhance our own well-being.

Let the positivity from your soul spread in the universe and come back to you in abundance!

04

YOGA AND MEDITATION

Have you noticed how even the smallest of things seem to trouble us these days? We get irritated by insignificant things, and as a result we are unable to deal with the many problems in our personal and professional lives. The reason behind this is the lack of control we have over ourselves. It hampers our mood and intervenes with our daily functioning. When we feel low for a long time, our bodies become more fragile and vulnerable to diseases.

The mind and body are totally distinct. However, they unquestionably influence one another. We are all aware that it is vital to care for our physical bodies so that we look and feel good. However, taking care of our mind is equally important. But how does one do it?

The answer lies with yoga and meditation.

The term yoga is derived from the Sanskrit root word *yuj,* which means to connect, attach, or join. Hence, yoga is the connection between our soul and the divine, which helps us in achieving spiritual awakening, i.e., higher consciousness and equilibrium in life.[24]

The sage Patanjali, who is considered the author of *Yoga Sutra,* and the Buddha both guaranteed that meditation could remove the agony brought about by an untamed human mind. They encouraged their followers to develop alertness, compassion, and delight. They accepted that it was conceivable to change one's psychological forces and patterns of emotion by consistently practising meditation.[25]

Both yoga and meditation help in bridging the gap between our mind and body, enabling them to work in harmony. Once both mind and body are aligned, everything else falls into place.

Meditation is to the mind what physical exercise is to the body. It takes charge of the mind and trains it to become more attentive, aware, mindful and achieve an intellectually clear and emotionally calm, stable state.[26] We truly agree with Ajahn Brahm, who said, 'Meditation is like a gym in which you develop the powerful mental muscles of calm and insight.'

Yoga helps increase flexibility, agility, weight loss, and toning along with muscle strength. It also improves metabolism, sleep quality, blood flow and functioning of respiratory and cardiovascular systems.[27] A report by the Fred Hutchinson Cancer Research Center states that individuals who practise yoga are progressively more careful about what they eat and thus less likely to be obese.[28]

This powerful duo of yoga and meditation can significantly change your journey through life. It can improve your connection with yourself and the ones around you. Performing yoga and meditation is like learning any other skill. Consider it like practising a muscle that you've never truly worked out before. It takes regular practice to get settled. In fact, we've made it even simpler for you to understand in our *Hatha Yoga* workbook. Not only will you be able to take charge of yourself and your health, you will also start experiencing a healthy, peaceful, and rewarding life.

So let yourself loose and create your own calm. Break free of your personal prison and find freedom.

05

DAILY EXERCISE REGIMEN

Just as a plant can't survive on sunlight only, our body can't survive merely on food. While it is a very important component to healthy living, human beings are complex creatures and there are other vital needs that are required to live well. One such need, whose importance I cannot stress enough, is exercise. Exercising on a regular basis boosts your immune system, burns calories, makes you feel better and more self-confident, and helps improve efficiency at work.

A good workout in the morning can do wonders for your body. It strengthens your muscles, enhances your endurance, helps you manage your weight, combats various health risks, and clears your mind, making you psychologically and physically sound. Exercise involves a lot of physical activity, thereby releasing feel-good hormones such as serotonin and endorphins, relieving stress, and making you feel relaxed, happy, and energetic.

Surprising Health Benefits of Exercising Regularly[29]

- Regular workouts protect you from various chronic diseases, as well as decreases the likelihood of contracting cardiovascular diseases.
- Regular exercising enhances our mood, which further results in better interpersonal relationships.
- It is important to exercise for a better sex life as it increases the blood flow, enhances flexibility and efficiency of the cardiovascular system in both men and women and decreases incidents of erectile dysfunction in men.
- It enables one to have sound sleep. The energy consumed during workout is recuperated during sleep, which improves the

quality of sleep.

- Exercising has been shown to improve one's brain health, the executive functioning of the brain, such as one's memory.
- Regular exercise helps to reduce pain and also increases tolerance to pain.
- Exercise improves one's skin quality as it can increase the blood flow in all parts of the body. This allows the skin to breathe properly, as well as produce natural antioxidants that make you look young and beautiful.

Most people know the benefits of exercising regularly, but many face challenges in actually doing it. This is where the idea of breaking one's own barrier comes into play. Don't look at others and compare yourself to them, as you are two different individuals with unique traits.

Key points that can help you while following your schedule

- **Track your progress:** Make sure you keep track of how far you have to go. It will keep you motivated to exercise every day.
- **Make your workout fun:** Put on your favourite music and lose yourself in it. Exercise to the beats.
- **Use props for exercising:** Use the "New Me" box, a medicine ball, frisbee, etc., as supporting tools or props.
- **Involve others:** Let your friends and family be a part of your fitness journey and you'll have one of the best experiences of your life.
- **Keep breaking your barriers:** Challenge yourself daily and keep striving for greater goals.

Kickstart your workout, set fitness goals for yourself, and earn yourself a good and healthy body, because let's not forget, "Good things come to those who sweat".

06

SEXUAL WELL-BEING

It is important to make sexual health part of your healthcare routine. Sexual health does not only mean having sexual intercourse; it means having a healthier body and mind as everything in our body is interdependent. Experiencing pleasure, intimacy, and joy is as important for our overall well-being as it is to maintain a healthy body.

A few important benefits of sexual well-being:

- Boosts your immune system.
- Helps you sleep better.
- Improves bladder control for women.
- Lowers blood pressure.
- You get a workout!
- Lowers the risk of a heart attack.

FRUITS THAT IMPROVE SEXUAL WELL-BEING NATURALLY

Pomegranate

Studies have shown that pomegranate juice can help improve erectile dysfunction. This fruit is packed with antioxidants that can increase testosterone levels, improve sperm quality, and increase sex drive. Have a glass of pomegranate juice daily and see the changes in your sexual health.[30]

Watermelon

It is a summer fruit known for its high water content. It is also known as a natural Viagra. Watermelons contain a non-essential amino acid called L-Citrulline. The body converts this to the essential amino acid, arginine, which is a precursor to nitric oxide. Nitric oxide is the compound responsible for dilating the blood vessels, resulting in lower blood pressure and better blood flow.[31]

Figs

Figs are given a lot of importance in India to treat digestive as well as reproductive health issues. They are said to contain aphrodisiac properties, which makes them an important food to increase sexual well-being. The fruit is a fine source of magnesium and potassium. Both of these minerals are essential to sexual performance. Dietary fiber is key not only to maintaining a healthy weight and heart health, but also to help you feel your most sexy.[32]

Avocado

Avocado contains vitamin B6, which some studies show can decrease symptoms of premenstrual syndrome (such as fatigue, bloating, and irritability). This might make it easier for women to 'get in the mood.'[33]

NATURAL HERBS FOR IMPROVING SEXUAL WELL-BEING:

Ashwagandha

A very popular herb in Ayurveda, ashwagandha has become popular around the world for its benefits to improve immunity, regulating stress, and increasing concentration levels and energy. Cortisol, a hormone, is physiologically released in response to stress. This becomes problematic when stress is persistent and cortisol levels become chronically elevated. Both cortisol and testosterone are made from the same precursor in the body, therefore, a high demand for cortisol will have a negative impact on testosterone production. This explains how stress can affect your libido, energy, weight gain, and mood. The good news is that ashwagandha can also reduce cortisol levels.[34]

Shatavari

It is believed to be one of the most powerful aphrodisiacs present in nature. It is known for improving sexual function by increasing the blood circulation, thus improving erectile dysfunction. It also plays a major role in improving the quality as well as density of sperm.

Tribulus

Tribulus terrestris or Gokhru/Gokhshura is a small leafy plant, the roots and fruit of which are popular in traditional Chinese as well as Ayurvedic medicine. It is also widely available as a sports supplement and commonly marketed to boost testosterone levels and improve sex drive.

Fenugreek (Methi)

Fenugreek is a popular herb in alternative medicine that may help in enhancing libido and improve sexual function. It is believed to contain compounds that your body uses to produce sex hormones, such as estrogen and testosterone. It is a commonly used herb in Indian cooking.

It is believed that fenugreek interacts with blood-thinning medications, such as warfarin. If you're on a blood thinner, you should speak with your medical practitioner before consuming fenugreek.

Saffron

Saffron is a delicious spice derived from the Crocus sativus flower. Its many traditional uses range from reducing stress to acting as an aphrodisiac.

Shilajit

Shilajit is known to boost libido and energy levels, which is why it features as a top herb for sexual health problems. Used since ancient times, shilajit can also be used for premature ejaculation and other sexual health disorders.[35]

Flax Seeds

Phytoestrogens are a form of dietary estrogen we get from food. Studies indicate they can enhance the natural hormone's health benefits. Flax seeds have a healthy amount of phytoestrogens. They can be particularly beneficial for women who have low estrogen levels and even those who may be experiencing menopause. Ground flax seeds are also rich in omega-3 fatty acids and L-arginine, which further boost libido.

They are easy to sprinkle on many dishes. You can bake flax seeds into bread and cookies, or blend them into smoothies and spreads.

Raisins

Raisins are packed with many essential nutrients. Raisins are rich in Vitamin A, selenium, potassium, iron and Vitamin B, and they also contain high levels of arginine and polyphenolic phytonutrients. These nutrients play an important role in keeping an individual sexually active and thriving.

However, sexual desire is complex and has to do with many more factors than just nutrition, like an individual's relationships, stress level, and personal preferences. It is natural for people to experience ups and downs in their interest in sex. But a feeling of lost desire for a long period of time must be taken seriously. Follow *The New Me* religiously for 90 days to see a drastic change, not only in your physical and mental health, but also in your sexual health.

07

BREAK YOUR OWN BARRIERS

What do you see when you look into a mirror? The person that you see is your only competition. Yes, you are your biggest competition. You are your biggest critic, motivator and supporter. The sooner you realize that, the better it is. We are not in a race to compete against each other, but to push ourselves to be better every day. And in order to do that, it is important that we break our own barriers.

It is a very simple yet effective formula. All you have to do is keep pushing yourself, adding to the work from the day before. Do 2-5 push-ups more than you did yesterday. If you run 500 metres one day, add a 100m the next. Once you start doing this, you will realize you are able to accomplish much more in the same amount of time than what you would have done earlier. And if we multiply it by 30 days, you will be amazed to see an exponential growth in your own potential. Your progress graph will shoot up like a skyscraper, making you feel motivated and energized.

Do not set unrealistic goals when you first begin a new diet or a new workout regimen. It is not practical to put yourself under too much pressure and attempt rigorous training you aren't prepared for. This is why the concept of breaking your own barriers comes into play. It helps you strengthen your body and spirit. It focusses on taking one step at a time and empowers you to break the boundaries you have created around yourself.

Let's take an easy example. If you abruptly start running for 5 kilometres without having built the endurance required for it, then within a day or two, your body will give up. You'll feel sore and exhausted as a result of exceeding your capabilities. The difference between the amount of energy consumed and the amount of energy expended will also make you irritable. Just as nutrition requirements vary from individual to individual, so does exercise. It depends on various factors such as diet, fitness goals, gender, and other specific situations.

This theory of consistently pushing oneself helps an individual go the extra mile while also taking their physical capacity into consideration. You will be surprised to see how easy it is to consistently keep going, with small increases, and achieve what you previously considered impossible.

Let us put in the effort to build a better version of ourselves. Effort and intention have to be calibrated and implemented in a positive direction. Start today, start small, but take the first step and don't look back. Keep moving forward. This strategy can be implemented not only in your workout, but in your personal and professional lives as well, empowering you to achieve your dreams.

Everyone gets opportunities, but one needs to learn how to take advantage of them. Decide your goals and harness your will power to break your own barriers and you will become unstoppable.

In essence:

1. Start with small and realistic goals.
2. Add small amounts of 'extra' every day.
3. Compete against yourself – what you were yesterday against what you are today.

08

POWER OF POSITIVITY

'You change, the world will change.' A straightforward statement, yet one that has exceptionally profound importance.

The only thing under our control is our own self. We can't make others do what we feel like, or think the way we want them to think. The only person you can control is yourself and that is one of the most powerful things we can possess. As soon as we gain control over our thoughts and actions, we can conquer anything.

Thoughts hold power

A thought is a very powerful weapon. It can either make you or break you, depending on how you use it. Thus, everything you do now affects your future. Every action that you take today constructs your future. In a way, our thoughts create our reality. If you look closely, we have always been given choices – choices like making excuses and blaming others, or getting back up and making the most of our situation.

If we want something we have never had, we have to do something we have never done. A famous saying by Chinese philosopher Lao Tzu goes, 'Watch your thoughts, they become your words; watch your words, they become your actions; watch your actions, they become your habits; watch your habits, they become your character; watch your character, it becomes your destiny.'

Let's take a very practical example of the power of our minds. Say, you visit a doctor and are told there are chances you might have diabetes in the next six months. After hearing this, there are two types of reactions you can have. The first is you heed his words as the final result, take on a lot of stress but take zero action against

it. Six months later, you get diabetes. The second possibility is that upon hearing the news, you change your attitude and diet, and exercise regularly, causing a positive change in your life. In the above example, we see that two different reactions can result in two different outcomes.
When we pre-decide something – good or bad – we inadvertently manifest that particular experience in the way we have imagined.

After all, life is all energy.

Things only pan out when our thoughts are aligned with our beliefs. We can have any number of thoughts, but it only holds meaning when we attach our belief to it. When you place 100 per cent of your faith and belief in something and your actions towards it are persistent, it becomes real, it becomes concrete.

Manifestation

When you believe in something and when you truly want something, you intentionally or unintentionally take action towards it and discover a way to get there. You make it happen. Let us see how to remain positive.

- Negative thoughts such as hatred or anger against anyone or anything harm us more than they harm others. Similarly, positive thoughts towards others can bring positivity into your life.
- Consciously remind yourself each morning that 'today is going to be the best day'.
- Each time you find yourself overthinking! stop. Redirect your thoughts towards some work.
- Set reminders for every 1 or 2 hours in your phone, to THINK POSITIVELY. After every reminder, take a minute to replace negative thoughts with positive ones. If you follow this, you'll soon be filled with positive thoughts and eventually won't need any more reminders as positivity will come naturally to you.

- If any unpleasant thing happens to you, try and list three reasons how that thing helped you or what you learnt from it.
- Turn your worries into prayers.
- Have faith that you'll get everything that you have ever dreamt. Leave no room for any kind of doubts.
- Every day, thank god or the universe and show gratitude for everything that you have and in everything that you do.
- Everything that you start – be it a new business, a new job, a college, or a relationship – always start with positivity and with faith in yourself.
- Focus on the good things.
- Practice positive self-talk.
- Focus on solutions and any action that you can take to calm down.
- Never give up.

Thoughts are like mirrors; what you think, manifests. Thus, if you want to see yourself as beautiful, you must first believe that you are beautiful.

And always remember: warriors lose a battle only when they stop fighting it.

09

CLUB 99 OR 99 KA FER

Are you a member of Club 99? Don't know what it is? Let's find out!

Greed is the assumption that it is all for my consumption.
-Andy Stanley

There was once a piece of land. The landlord told a prospective farmer, 'I'll give you as much land as you can walk around in, in one day.' The farmer's eyes gleamed with eagerness and greed, and he started running. He ran so much, and so far, that he eventually collapsed and died of exhaustion.

People strain their mind, body and soul throughout their lives because they are not satisfied with their current situation.
Everything is right only when done within limits. An excess of anything is not good.

The Story of Club 99

Once, a king sat in the balcony of his palace along with a minister. Beyond the wall of the palace lived a poor family. They were happy and would laugh a lot. They were content.

The king couldn't understand how they could be happy despite such poverty. The minister hatched a plan to explain it to the king. He left a bundle of 99 gold coins at the doorstep of this poor family.

When the family returned from their daily job, they found that small bundle. The man picked it up and saw that it was full of money. But the amount was 99, not 100. So in order to round it up to a nice 100, they decided to add to it. They felt that that's when they would be truly happy. The man and his wife stopped eating one meal a day. Night or day, they began to save enough to add one more gold coin. They slowly began to stop interacting, or even eating together. Over time, they began to lose interpersonal contentment and also their peace of mind.

After a few months, the minister happened to ask the king if he could still hear laughter from the hut. The king said that he couldn't.

99 ka fer had got the family in its trap; they no longer laughed or had time for each other.

Some people are overly obsessed with the concept of growing their wealth. So as soon as their money reaches 99, they have this intense urge to make it 100, and get trapped in this vicious cycle. Sometimes, it gets so addictive that in some cases they are ready to put their needs, families and even themselves at stake. There is a very subtle difference between ambition and greed. People often don't realize when they've surpassed the line and have started acquiring selfish desires for money, power, status, and such. It's a deadly trap, and we all must reflect on our intent time and again to make sure that we maintain a balance between our thoughts and actions. We must pursue everything with pure intentions and determination. It is only then that we'll be able to achieve success.

In order to counter what I call 'the club 99', one requires balance in life, and the key to achieving balance is contentment.

Contentment is a state of mind where the individual is satisfied with things as they are while working for the better. It is a conscious effort to appreciate, accept, and enjoy what one already has. It not only gives you peace and happiness, but also saves you from a lot of useless expenditure, eventually creating healthy relationships with oneself and others.

You might question why we first discussed working hard and striving for change, and now we are talking about being satisfied. Satisfaction can come only once we are settled comfortably in a situation. To get there, we need a healthy mind and body. We are striving to help you get there.

What happens if you wear the same jacket for years without any care? It tears. In the same way, excessive pressure on your body also causes wear and tear. Taking this into consideration, we encourage you to work according to your individual capacity.

There is a thin line between being content and being complacent. One is healthy, and the other is not. Contentment means that you are happy with what you have at the moment, yet open for exploration. A complacent individual provides unreasonable excuses for not working and doesn't work to reach their maximum potential.

"Contentment makes poor men rich, discontentment makes rich men poor." — Benjamin Franklin

Let's visualize Discontentment v/s Contentment

In case of discontentment, one possesses many things while lacking the awareness to appreciate them. This leads to a huge discrepancy between the things one has and the things one wants, making an individual upset and causing them to feel miserable all the time.

DISCONTENTMENT

CONTENTMENT

Whereas, on the contrary, a content person keeps a balance of the two, i.e. he/she enjoys what he/she already has and simultaneously works towards his/her growth.

How to develop contentment unconsciously

- **Gratitude:** After waking up, list out five things that you're grateful for. For example: your parents or family, an able body or even the new day itself. You'll realize that you are so fortunate.
- **No comparisons**: Make sure you don't compare yourself with anyone because no one showcases their failures. So it's important for you to remember that you are unique and you have a purpose. Don't let your skill and talent go to waste. Make conscious efforts to think about the things you are good at. You'll be surprised to see that gradually, the unwanted thoughts will fade away.
- **Train your mind to see the beauty:** For many of us, it is easy to point out our weaknesses, but we struggle when we are asked to identify our strengths. Practise seeing the beauty that exists around you, and focus on your positives.
- **Random acts of kindness:** A famous Chinese proverb goes: 'If you want happiness for an hour, take a nap. If you want happiness for a day, go fishing. If you want happiness for a year, inherit a fortune. If you want happiness for a lifetime, help someone else.'

Research shows that if you help others selflessly, it not only uplifts you, but makes you healthier and more productive as well. Being generous is hardwired in the brain and is pleasurable just like food and sex.

- **Beauty sleep:** In order to improve your beauty sleep, internally as well as externally, think about at least three things (gradually you can increase the number) in your entire day which you found heartwarming or happy. It could be a kind gesture or something that you learnt.
- **Be content without getting complacent:** Be content with what you have and not with what you are. Learning is a lifelong process and need not necessarily be formal. Every day, try and learn something out of interest. Read a book, pick up a new hobby. As soon as you stop moving forward ,you start going backwards.

Extremes are easy. I dare you to strike a balance.

10

SELF-DISCIPLINE

Among all leading professionals, across various fields, there is one common ingredient for achieving success that doesn't often receive its fair share of the limelight – self-discipline.

Self-discipline is the essential ability of controlling oneself. It is of utmost importance and is yet an unpopular factor. Most people mistakenly equate this ability to a punishment or a rigid way of living.

Motivational speaker Jim Rohn says, we all must suffer one of two pains:

1. Pain of discipline
2. Pain of regret

The choice is yours to make. Choose wisely.

Self-discipline requires making correct decisions, against all odds. You've got to keep making that choice until you reach your goal because discipline is not a one-day affair; it's everyday practice. Whatever we practise becomes a habit. Have you ever thought why doing the right thing has always been tough?

Successful individuals practise discipline. We prefer immediate gratification of our desires. Most importantly, we focus on the things we want 'now' instead of focusing on the things we want most, things that take determination.

Self-discipline is equivalent to self-love. If you love and respect yourself enough, you'll be determined to make decisions based on your best interest.

It is time to turn thoughts into reality, replace doubts with faith and fear with possibilities. Believe me when I say you have immense potential waiting to be tapped.

Research shows that the human brain is 30 times more powerful than the IBM Sequoia, one of the world's fastest computers.[39] It is believed that even the smartest people in the world have utilized only 15 per cent of their brains. You yourself as a human are far superior to anything that exists in this world.

With this massive amount of power residing within you, you are capable of everything. You're capable of every thought you've ever had, every dream you've ever dreamt, no matter how lofty it may seem.

If you're ready to take on The New Me challenge, you'll be able to tap into and utilize your innate resources optimally. It may sound incredibly hard at first, but remember to 'start by doing small'. You don't need to push yourself completely and feel exhausted at the end. We're asking you to start small, one thing at a time, and eventually you'll get addicted to it once you start seeing the results.

So, if you've been wanting to shed those extra 20 pounds, start your workout now. If you've been procrastinating on that assignment, slog it out. If you're fearful of starting something big because you might end up failing, set achievable goals and pour your heart and soul into it. I bet there is nothing that can stop you from reaching great heights.

Motivation may fade, but it is your self-discipline that will keep you going.

SUCCESS STORY

BARACK OBAMA

(44th US President)

Obama is known for his simplistic, yet consistent, routine. He wakes up early every morning, works out, reads plenty of newspapers and then has his breakfast with his family. He focusses on what is crucial, stays focused, and takes only necessary decisions. He works well into the evenings, but always makes time to have dinner with the family. He sets a perfect example of a balanced, simplistic, and focused routine.

11

SAY NO TO TOBACCO

Do you think there is anything worse than losing control over yourself? Cigarettes, drugs, or habit forming substances make you a mere puppet in the hands of others. Getting sloshed and taking pictures with a cigarette in your hands may seem 'cool' and aspirational in the moment, but the long-term effects of addiction have nothing cool about it.

Not being in control of one's senses is one of the most unattractive things a person can do. What is attractive is hard work, never giving up, and taking charge of yourself and your situation.

We live in a world where we display more than what we have, we try and impress people we barely know because we're trying to fit in and need validation from others. Sometimes, it is only because of peer pressure.

All of us are aware of the harm caused by the consumption of drugs, cigarettes, and other such substances. We know consuming them is no better than directly attacking our lungs, liver, and heart. People work hard throughout their lives so that they can enjoy their retirement. Nobody wants to go through pain and suffering or spend their savings on hospital bills.I am sure all of us have either seen, or are aware of, examples of how addiction has ruined people's lives, their families, and their relationships over time. It is very disheartening that people are unaware of the actual meaning of life and that they lose their way indulging in such unimportant and self-sabotaging things.

Tobacco and drugs are like slow poisons. They don't kill you immediately. They don't give you an easy death, and they'll suck

all the energy out of you, gradually taking away your health, relationships, finances, and leave an empty husk of you. Some people learn in time, whereas others don't, and hence suffer.

In his book *The Monk Who Sold His Ferrari,* author Robin Sharma talks about a crisis he found himself in where he almost lost his life, from a heart attack, due to smoking. After the incident he came to India and became a monk. After his near-death experience, he realized that life was much more than just indulging in one's vices and creating stress.

We are unaware of what is expected out of us. Such indulgences serve as a bait, due to which people lose sight of their original path and meaning of life. Don't get trapped in it. Keep striving to achieve your goals. There will be many tests on your journey, so stay focused. When you say no to smoking, tobacco, and drugs, you are saying yes to a healthy lifestyle.

Here is what you can do for yourself

- **Find the purpose of your life:** Find the actual meaning of life. Figure out what makes you happy and pursue it with all your heart.
- **Believe that you can and you will:** Have faith that you have the will power to stop something unpleasant and the strength to overcome your challenges.
- **Start by achieving small goals:** Start by refraining for a couple of hours a day, gradually increasing it to whole day, and then ultimately quitting.
- **Celebrate small successes:** Give small treats or rewards whenever you move closer to your goals. No matter how small the move is, always appreciate yourself.
- **Keep a track of your progress:** Keep recording your progress. That will keep you motivated.

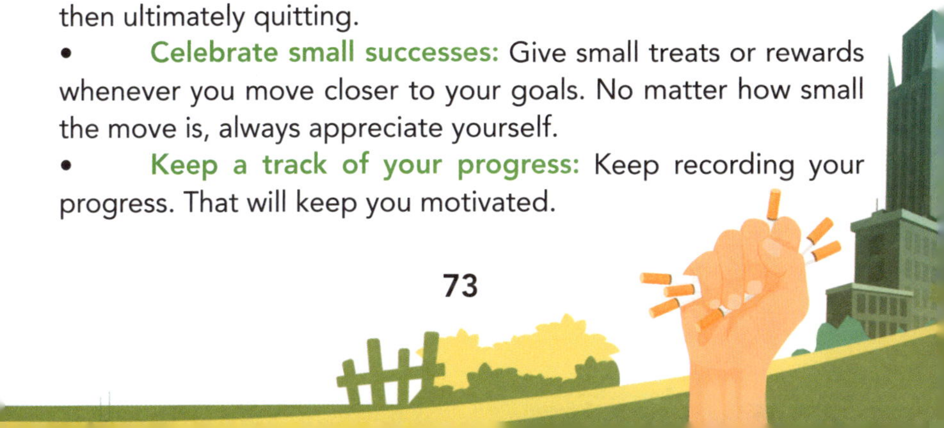

'If you can quit for a day, you can quit for a lifetime.'

Benjamin Alire Saenz

12

WEIGHT LOSS

The most used yet the least applied quote, 'health is wealth', needs to be taken seriously and applied to our lifestyle. No amount of money can help us if we don't have our mind, body, or soul in the right place.

It is indeed important to love ourselves, but that does not mean we accept the imbalance in our body – for it may be something that could harm us. Loving yourself means you take care of yourself, both mentally and physically. It is important to weed out the root cause of the problem rather than just alter our feelings and say, for instance, 'I love however I am'. It is okay to love yourself, but not when you have the power to change for the better. We must make efforts to get better each day.

There is no such thing as 'healthy obese'. Did you know that just by losing weight you can prevent the risk of many potentially serious health conditions like strokes and type-2 diabetes?[36]

As the saying goes, 'you are what you eat'. Our mood and eating patterns go hand in hand. If we fix our eating patterns, we can positively impact our emotional state as well. Thus, it is important to eat healthy and nutritious meals in order to feel good internally.

Obesity is associated with various health risks. It makes one more susceptible to high blood pressure, an increase in cholesterol levels, which thereby may lead to various diseases such as cancer, heart and gall-bladder diseases, osteoarthritis, body pains, gout, and various breathing problems.

How can you tell if you are overweight?

• Body Mass Index (BMI)

One way of finding out is through the Body Mass Index (BMI), which categorises the individual in underweight, normal, overweight and extremely overweight categories based on our weight and height.

$$\text{BMI} = \frac{\text{Weight (kg)}}{\text{Height (m}}$$

WEIGHT CATEGORIES	BMI (Kg/m^2)
Underweight	<18.5
Healthy Weight	18.5-24.9
Overweight	25-29.9
Obese	30-34.9
Severely Obese	35-39.9
Morbidly Obese	>40

• Health Numbers

Another way of checking is to keep the values given below within their limits.

MEASURE	TARGET
Target BMI	18.5-24.9
Blood Pressure	120/80 mm Hg or less
LDL (bad cholesterol)	Less than 100 mg/dl
HDL (good cholesterol)	Men: more than 40 mg/dl Women: more than 50 mg/dl
Triglycerides	Less than 150 mg/dl
Blood sugar (fasting)	Less than 100 mg/dl

It is important to look after our bodies and to fight a preventive battle against some of the most common causes of death. *The New Me* is a catalyst in your journey to lose excess weight. It will surely motivate you to adopt a healthy lifestyle through various positive reinforcements and continual assistance.

In the modern world, where technology is taking over, the average individual's lifestyle has become increasingly sedentary, which makes having the right dietary intake and regular physical activity all the more important. Maintaining your weight helps you to decrease the risk of diseases, boosts self-esteem, builds confidence, improves sleeping patterns, cleanses the body (making you glow from within) and enhances interpersonal relationships.[37]

Let's revamp ourselves, and three months from now, you will thank yourself for having started what you once thought was impossible.

Your body is your temple. Make it your top priority. It's not selfish. It is necessary.

Here is one exercise for you.

Q1. How do you feel about yourself?

Q2. List down some ways in which you can improve yourself.

Q3. How would you feel having achieved everything mentioned above?

Let nothing hold you back!

You may not know this yet,
but you have the ability to
reinvent yourself endlessly.
That's your beauty.

Linda Yuknavitch

13

IT'S WITHIN YOU

There is a voice within each of us that knows what is good for us and what is not. No matter how much we resist listening to it, we know it is there. Doing the wrong thing can be easy, but it takes enormous courage to abide by the right and the ethical choices. Our present is a reflection of our past choices.

The question then arises, are we willing to do what is right? It may seem daunting at first, but the sense of accomplishment and fearlessness that you get when you commit is incomparable. You have the strength to complete any task that is presented to you. You have the potential to carry out each and every one of your dreams. You possess all the power that you need and the courage that you require. Doing what's right sets you free from the shackles of failure.

When you start doing the right thing, you will feel the addiction to always do it that way. It is you who has the power to control your mind and work on it.

The most successful and happy people are those who understand this, and can instruct their mind to do what they want it to do, and not get distracted by the negativity that surrounds them. You too have the power to think positively and work on yourself and commit to everything, not just in this workbook, but in life.

Life is short and unpredictable. We don't know what's going to happen tomorrow, but what we can do is try our best today and keep giving it our all every day. Let self-discipline guide you and consistently follow this 90-day routine and seize the day.

You know yourself better than anyone. You know your strengths and weaknesses and how to mould them to your benefit. You are aware of what will enable you to commit to the schedule for the next 3 months.

The feeling of achieving the milestones you set for yourself is inexplicable. When you start walking down this path of health and success, you wouldn't want to throw it away. Once you convince yourself to create a better, more organized, powerful and healthier you, then nothing can stop you from achieving it.

Start acknowledging the immense potential that you have and activate your powers to become the New You. So invest your time in things you would want to grow. Act on it and make the impossible possible. Let the world wonder how you brought about such a massive change in your life and don't turn back because, as Hellen Keller once stated, 'We can do anything we want to do if we stick to it long enough.'

SUCCESS STORY

STEVE JOBS

(Co-Founder of Apple Computers)

Steve Jobs always emphasized one thing: Always love what you do! He was an enterprising legend. He began Apple in a garage with Steve Wozniak in 1976 after he dropped out of college.[38] He was perhaps the most youthful individual to be highlighted on the Forbes rundown of the nation's most extravagant individuals – a major accomplishment without the support of any family riches.

After he was terminated from the Macintosh gathering, he went on to build his new organization, NeXT.[39] However, he couldn't cope because of the significant expenses of the machines.

He then tried to revamp his already existing company, Pixar Animation Studio, which went on to become a huge success. He returned as the Apple CEO and restored the organization back to its initial achievement. Although he passed away in 2011, his legacy continues. [40]

Jobs' life is a demonstration of how disappointments open new opportunities.

14

THE BEST WHO CHANGED THE GAME

Professional athletes don't reach the peak by either luck or accident. It takes disciple and superhuman levels of dedication, focus, and time. What's of utmost importance is what they eat. In this chapter, we take a look at some world-class athletes across the world who have changed their diet and as a result, feel better, stronger, faster, and more energetic than ever before.

Dotsie Bausch was a 26-year-old fashion model who was struggling with eating disorders and drug addiction. One day, during a therapy session, her therapist encouraged her to take up a physical activity. Something that was not attached to any goal of fitness. She chose cycling. She loved it so much that she became serious about it and it eventually led her to take up competitive cycling. She rose to the top at an age when most athletes had already established their careers.

It was during her training for the 2012 London Olympics that she started a plant-based diet and lifestyle. She noticed that within the first 10 days of going plant-based, she woke up feeling lighter and definitely more energetic. At the age of 40, she won a silver medal in Women's Track Cycling, establishing a record for the competition.

As a professional cyclist, Dotsie has 8 US national championships, two Pan-American gold medals, including a silver medal at the 2012 London Olympics, under her belt.

You'd think German Strongman Patrik Baboumian's diet is all about consuming plentiful meat and eggs. But, Baboumian could not be more different.

He was named Germany's Strongest Man in 2011. This was also the year when he decided to move from a vegetarian diet to a completely plant-based diet. Since then, he has picked up victories in powerlifting. He won the European Powerlifting Championships in 2012, and also set 4 world records along the way.

According to Toronto's festival organizers, Baboumian shouldered the heaviest load ever, one that is equivalent to a large horse. 'It's a bit stupid to do things like that, it really hurts,' Baboumian said to the festival audience, as reported by the Toronto Star. 'But, the point is to inspire people and break stereotypes that tough guys need to eat a lot of meat.'[41]

Today, the 40-year-old athlete has competed in and won several weightlifting and strongman competitions during his career, and even broken world records.

Pro tennis player Venus Williams was diagnosed with the autoimmune disease Sjögren's Syndrome in 2011. This disease causes joint pain and fatigue.

Williams' future in tennis looked precarious. Transitioning to a no-animal-products or produce diet, however, changed the game.

The seven-time Grand Slam Champion says that a plant-based lifestyle allowed her to manage her condition without medicine. It also improved her skin.[42]

British professional boxer David Haye turned to a plant-based diet after an injury that was taking long to heal. He said: 'All roads kept leading back to a plant-based diet.'

There is a strong misconception that in strength or combat sports, people will suddenly become protein deficient if they give up meat or dairy. But Gary Turner – a 13-time world champion sportsman – said in an interview that athletes can get all the protein they need from a diet that does not involve animals in any form, if they eat according to caloric needs.[43]

The multiple world championship winner says he found out that a plant- based diet gave him performance benefits. The British boxer, also known as 'the Haymaker' says, 'I've not had cheese or milk for the last two years and I've felt the benefits from that .... Since cutting out meat, I've felt healthier, cleaner, lighter. My skin, my nails and hair, I stopped getting dandruff, there are loads of really positive effects I got from that.'

When people asked him where he got his strength from, he said: 'Where does an ape get his strength from? [Apes are] 20 times stronger than humans and they don't rely on a meat-based diet. They eat plants all day long. It's a myth that you need meat for strength.[44]

The multiple gold medalist in the disability section, Heather Mills is known to be one of the leading athletes globally in the sport of downhill skiing. She suffered the loss of part of her leg in 1993 when she was involved in a collision with a police motorcycle. It had left her with a punctured lung and loss of the left leg 15 cm below the knee.

She says, 'I'd spent months in hospital with a leg infection. I was told if the infection did not heal I would have to lose my knee, so I was prepared to try anything. This led me to natural healing at the Hippocrates institute in Florida 1993.'

With only plants on her plate, the infection suddenly improved and rapid advancements were made in her healing process. Heather describes the dietary change as the 'springboard' to her recovery. She swears by the medical benefits of a no-meat or dairy diet. She is also outspoken about the animal cruelty aspect. She holds the world record for the fastest disabled woman on skis, reaching a top speed of 103.6 miles per hour in 2015.

Kendrick Farris, an Olympic weightlifter and record-holder, switched to a diet free of any animal products in 2014.

Farris went on a diet conversion before the birth of his second son because he wanted to set an example for him. He also credits eating plant-based with helping him recover faster and being more focused.

Farris said, 'I don't necessarily trust the way the food is being processed.[45] I don't agree with the way the animals are mass-slaughtered. So that's one thing that kind of got me looking at what they call a vegan diet.'

With meat off the menu, Farris, who competes in the 94 kg division, eats a lot of plant-based nutrition.

Farris has noticed a difference in his training and performance. 'Now, my body recovers a lot faster… I feel lighter. My mind is a lot more clear. I feel I can focus a lot better.' That focus helped him set a US record of a combined 377 kg at the Olympic trials in May, with a 209-kg clean-and-jerk and 168-kg snatch.[46]

Scott Jurek, the Ultramarathoner made headlines when he ran the entire length of the Appalachian Trail in a record-setting 46 days, 8 hours and 7 minutes. He's also won the 135-mile Badwater Ultramarathon, the 'world's toughest foot race,' twice; the 153-mile long Spartathlon in Greece three consecutive times; and has secured first place in just about all the world's ultrarunning high-profile races.

For Jurek, food has been a vital part of his life. In fact, his memoir is entitled *Eat & Run*. He has been on a no-animal/animal product diet since 1999.[47]

He eased into it starting in college, cutting out meat, then fish and then finally giving up all animal products completely. The decision was encouraged by a family history of chronic disease, including his mother's multiple sclerosis.

Jurek, now in his 40s, credits his diet for the length of his career and also his faster recovery time and lack of injuries. [48]

Lewis Hamilton has been following a plant-based diet since 2017. He has explained how following this diet has benefited him, especially his energy levels. He says that moving to a plant-based diet has been a 'life changer'.

'I have more energy; I'm so much more productive,' says Hamilton. 'I wake up feeling way better, clearer in thought and fresher in my body. I recover quicker; I sleep better. My skin cleared up. I have fewer allergies. There are just so many impacts.'

'I'm physically in better shape than I've ever been, and I'm more successful than ever right now, and my plant-based programme has played such a big role in that.' [49]

Challenging the myth that meat is needed to fuel a body to be fast and strong, Australian sprinter Morgan Mitchell turned plant-based in 2014 when she just 'dropped everything instantly' and calls the decision to quit all animal products including dairy as a 'weird light bulb moment.'[50] The Austprofessional sprinter became an Olympian in 2016 at the age of 21.

Powered by plants, she noticed many health improvements after making the switch. She said: 'I recover a lot quicker than I used to. It's easier to keep my weight down and I haven't been sick at all!'[51]

Known as a rule breaker who keeps pushing her limits, Mitchell swears that her no-meat or diary diet has helped her to see 'greater results on the track.' [52]

DR. MICHAEL GREGER

When Dr Michael Greger was a child, his grandmother, who had end-stage heart disease, was given a certain time to live. At the age of 65, his grandma had already undergone multiple heart bypass surgeries for clogged arteries.

She was stuck in a wheelchair and had chest pain.

Then one day his grandma saw a news story on TV about Nathan Pritikin, a man who ran health centers, claiming to reverse heart disease through a plant-based diet and exercise. She rolled into one of these centers on a wheelchair, and within 3 weeks she was walking miles every day. She ended up living to the age of 96.

That inspired Dr Greger to aim for medicine from a young age. As he says in his book, he 'made it my life's mission to find out' more about disease related to diet. He is a strong advocate of a plant-based diet and has also written the famous book *How Not to Die* in which he specifies plant-based foods that help you to live a long and healthy life.

KEY TAKEAWAYS

- Drink water once you wake up.
- Don't forget to make your bed.
- Have a hearty breakfast.
- Every morning, decide that today is going to be an awesome day!
- The only thing worse than a bad workout is no workout (based on your preference you may select exercise, yoga or a combination of both).
- Dress smart.
- Wear a smile and steal the show.
- Eat healthy snacks at appropriate times.
- Take time to have lunch at a peaceful place.
- Detox your thoughts and replenish yourself with positivity.
- Compliment/appreciate a minimum of three people every day.
- Fuel your body with a healthy dinner.
- Use your commuting time to listen to inspirational podcasts or positive videos.
- List three new things that you learn every day.
- List three good things that you do every day, no matter how small they may be.
- Say no to tobacco, smoking, and drugs.
- Always remember, it's only you who can help yourself, nobody else can do it for you.
- Everything that you are seeking is already within you.
- Take care of yourself first in order to take care of the outside world.

RECOMMENDED READING

- *The Monk Who Sold His Ferrari* by Robin Sharma
- *Autobiography of a Yogi* by Yogi Yoganand
- *How Not to Die* by Dr Michael Greger
- *The Secret* by Rhonda Byrne
- *You Can Heal Your Life* by Louise Hay

REFERENCES

1 'Sleep, Learning, and Memory.' Sleep, Learning, and Memory | Healthy Sleep, healthysleep.med.harvard.edu/healthy/matters/benefits-of-sleep/ learning-memory.

2 Davis, Nicola. 'How Does the Body Clock Work?' The Guardian, Guardian News and Media, 18 Sept. 2013, www.theguardian.com/science/2013/ sep/18/body-clock-jet-lag.

3 Montag, Ali. 'This Is Billionaire Jeff Bezos' Daily Routine and It Sets Him up for Success.' CNBC, CNBC, 15 Sept. 2018, www.cnbc.com/2018/09/14/ billionaire-jeff-bezos-shares-the-daily-routine-he-uses-to-succeed.html.

4 [https://www.health.harvard.edu/staying-healthy/how-much-water- should-you-drink]

5 Team, Family Health. 'How Healthy Eating Can Help You to Age Better.' Health Essentials from Cleveland Clinic, Health Essentials from Cleveland Clinic, 18 Feb. 2020, health.clevelandclinic.org/how-to-age-better-by- eating-more-healthfully/

6 'Benefits of a Balanced Diet.' World Health Organization, World Health Organization, 20 Mar. 2020, www.euro.who.int/en/health-topics/disease- prevention/nutrition/a-healthy-lifestyle/benefits-of-a-balanced-diet.

7 'The Importance of Eating Lunch - A Healthier Lifestyle: Provitamil - Great Tasting, Non-Dairy Alternatives to Milk & Soya.' Provitamil, www. provitamil.com/healthier-lifestyle/the-importance-of-eating-lunch.htm.

8 Chu, Wai Lang. 'Eating in Groups Makes Food Taste Better, Study Believes.' Foodnavigator.com, William Reed Business Media Ltd., 29 Feb. 2016, www.foodnavigator.com/Article/2016/02/29/Eating-in- groups- makes-food-taste-better-study-believes.

9 White, Susie. 'The Importance of Dinner.' Mental Healthy, www. mentalhealthy.co.uk/lifestyle/food/eating-for-good-mental-

health-dinner. html.
10 'The Top 10 Causes of Death.' World Health Organization, World Health Organization, www.who.int/news-room/fact-sheets/detail/the-top-10- causes-of-death.
11 'Causes of Death Statistics.' Census of India Website : Causes of Death Statistics, censusindia.gov.in/vital_statistics/causesofdeath.html.
12 SHARAN, sharan-india.org/.
13 Petre, Alina. '6 Science-Based Health Benefits of Eating Vegan.' Healthline, Healthline Media, 23 Sept. 2016, www.healthline.com/nutrition/ vegan-diet-benefits.
14 Greger, Michael, and Gene Stone. How Not to Die: Discover the Foods Scientifically Proven to Prevent and Reverse Disease. Pan Books, 2018.
15 'Go Vegan and Live Peacefully.' God Has Come, www.godhascome.com/go-vegan-and-live-peacefully/.
16 Definition of Veganism.' The Vegan Society, www.vegansociety.com/ go-vegan/definition-veganism.
17 '13 Myths about Veganism.' The Vegan Society, www.vegansociety. com/whats-new/blog/13-myths-about-veganism.
18 Vigoreaux, Gabriella. '54 Vegan Recipes so Good, You'll Forget About Meatand Cheese.' Good Housekeeping, 7 Nov. 2019, www.goodhousekeeping. com/food-recipes/healthy/g807/vegan-recipes/?slide=6.
19 13 Popular Fast-Food Menu Items That Are Surprisingly Perfect For Vegans.' Business Insider, www.businessinsider.in/13-popular-fast-food- menu-items-that-are-surprisingly-perfect-for-vegans/McDonalds-Fruit- and-maple-oatmeal-no-cream-and-apple-pie/slideshow/62855164.cms.
20 'A Multicenter Randomized Controlled Trial of a Plant-Based Nutrition Program to Reduce Body Weight and Cardiovascular Risk in the Corporate Setting: the GEICO Study.' European

Journal of Clinical Nutrition, Nature Publishing Group, July 2013, www.ncbi.nlm.nih.gov/pubmed/23695207.

21 Wilks, James, Pace, Joseph and Psihoyos Louie. The Game Changers. United States: Netflix, 2018.

22 'Animals Emotion Is Simple and Pure; Similarities between Animal and Autistic Emotion.' Livestock Behaviour, Design of Facilities and Humane Slaughter, www.grandin.com/inc/animals.in.translation.ch3.html.

23 Petter, Olivia. 'Going Vegan Is 'Single Biggest Way' to Reduce Our Impact on the Planet, Study Finds.' The Independent, Independent Digital News and Media, 29 Aug. 2018, www.independent.co.uk/life-style/health- and-families/veganism-environmental-impact-planet-reduced-plant- based-diet-humans-study-a8378631.html.

24 'Yoga Definition.' Parmarth Niketan, www.parmarth.org/yoga/yoga- definition/. Borohhov, Dmitri. 'Yoga- What Is Yoga?- Definition of the Sanskrit Word.' Ananda, 18 Nov. 2019,www.ananda.org/yogapedia/yoga/.

25 McGonigal, Kelly. 'The Big Brain Benefits of Meditation.' Yoga Journal, 1 June 2010, www.yogajournal.com/lifestyle/brain-meditation.

26 Gyalwa, Trungram. 'Benefits of Meditation for the Mind and Body.' Mindworks Meditation, 10 Apr. 2020, mindworks.org/blog/benefits- meditation-mind-body/.

27 'Benefits of Yoga.' American Osteopathic Association, www. osteopathic.org/what-is-osteopathic-medicine/benefits-of-yoga/

28 Kerr, Michael. 'Exercise and Weight Loss: Importance, Benefits & Examples.' Healthline, Healthline Media, 8 July 2017, www.healthline.com/ health/exercise-and-weight-loss.

29 'Benefits of Exercise.' MedlinePlus, U.S. National Library of Medicine, 4 Oct. 2019, medlineplus.gov/benefitsofexercise.

html.
30 https://www.thehealthsite.com/sexual-health/male-sexual-problems/ fruits-can-spice-up-your-sex-life-here-are-the-best-ones-for-you-717744/
31 https://www.bensnaturalhealth.com/blog/sexual-health/watermelon- natural-viagra/
32 https://www.eatsomethingsexy.com/aphrodisiac-foods/figs/
33 https: //www.pennmedicine .org/updates/blogs/health-and- wellness/2017/february/food-for-libido
34 https://www.marionguckclinic.com/blog/ashwaganda-health- benefits-for-men-libido-energy-more.html
35 https://www.india.com/lifestyle/erectile-dysfunction-here-are-some- herbs-to-your-rescue-3627845/
36 https://www.niddk.nih.gov/health-information/weight-management/ health-risks-overweight 'Health Risks of Being Overweight.' National Institute of Diabetes and Digestive and Kidney Diseases, U.S. Department of Health and Human Services, 1 Feb. 2015, www.niddk.nih.gov/health- information/weight-management/health-risks-overweight.
37 https://medshapeweightloss.com/emotional-benefits-of-losing- weight/#:~:text=In%20losing%20healthy%20weight%20you,can%20be%20 a%20huge%20stressor. '4 Emotional Benefits of Losing Weight: Blog: MedShape Weight Loss.' Medshape Weight Loss Clinics, 18 Oct. 2017,
38 CatClifford. 'Steve Jobs: These Are 2 Essential Ingredients for Success.' CNBC, 15 Nov. 2017, www.cnbc.com/2017/11/15/steve-jobs-bill-gates-how- to-be-successful.html.
39 Gupta, Sanchi. 'The Steve Jobs Success Story Is An Inspiration For Anyone Who Is Clueless Or Confused In Life.' ScoopWhoop, 24 Feb. 2017, www.scoopwhoop.com/steve-jobs-success-story/.

40 'Story of Strive: How Steve Jobs Found Success on the Road Less Traveled.' Scott Amyx, 30 Oct. 2017, scottamyx.com/2017/10/30/story- strive-steve-jobs-success/.

41 Vegan strongman shoulders 550 kg — a record, perhaps — at vegetarian food fest The Star]

42 [Edible Plants and Their Influence on the Gut Microbiome and Acne (nih.gov)]

43 What Is a Vegan Diet? a Guide for Getting Enough Nutrients (insider. com)]

44 https://www.businessinsider.com/how-to-eat-like-vegan-heavyweight- boxer-david-haye-2017-2?IR=T

45 Kendrick Farris, The Only Male U.S. Weightlifter In The Olympics, Is Totally Vegan | HuffPost Life.

46 Kendrick Farris sets U.S. record in Olympic Trials win (shreveporttimes. com).

47 https://www.sierraclub.org/sierra/2011-3-may-june/green-life/how- does-vegan-ultramarathoner-scott-jurek-do-it.

48 https://www.gq.com/story/the-real-life-diet-of-the-ultra-marathoner- who-gave-up-meat-and-became-vegan.

49 Lewis Hamilton: My Plant-Based Diet Makes Me More Successful - Longevity LIVE.

50 https://www.greatveganathletes.com/morgan-mitchell-vegan- sprinter/]

51 https://www.livekindly.co/olympian-morgan-mitchell-vegan/

52 https://www.wellandgood.com/vegan-athlete-protein-ideas/https:// www.freepik.com/.

Picture credits:

1. David Haye: The Sun
2. Venus Williams: Women's Tennis Association
3. Scott Jurek: Facebook
4. Patrik Baboumian: Great Vegan Athletes
5. Morgan Mitchell: The West Australian
6. Dr. Michael Greger: Wikimedia Commons
7. Lewis Hamilton: AutoSport
8. Kendrick Farris: Olympedia
9. Heather Mills: Digital spy
10. Dotsie Bausch: OMD blog
11. Digital artwork and vectors: Srishti Publishers

A few words from our happy readers...

"Gagan Dhawan has managed to curate a beautiful book on healthy living that can be easily adopted in our day-to-day lives."

"Very well researched and informative."

"A complete guide to lead a healthy and happy life."

"One of those books which has so much to give its readers. It is presented in a unique manner that the reader thoroughly enjoys reading it."

"It's a short read but the author has managed to convey a lot with this small book."

The healthier we keep, the better we eat and the more positive we think, the happier and more successful our lives are going to be. "THE NEW ME" provides concrete steps to be followed, a roadmap, to a healthy mind, body and soul. It is simple and practical to implement. If you follow this workbook religiously, success is guaranteed.

No matter what goals you set for yourself, this will help you achieve what previously felt unachievable in your life. You will experience the power of creating a healthier and happier life. It will get you unbelievable results both in your personal and professional life.

Instead of wasting time and giving excuses like
"I was busy" and "I'll do it later",
start investing in your body today!